The
LUCKY GIRL
JOURNAL

ALSO BY KEILA SHAHEEN

The Shadow Work Journal

The 369 Journal: Limitless Edition

The Vibrational Poetry Book

The
LUCKY GIRL
JOURNAL

*How Anyone Can Manifest
the Life of Their Dreams*

Keila Shaheen

PRIMERO
SUEÑO PRESS

ATRIA

New York   London   Toronto   Sydney   New Delhi

PRIMERO
SUEÑO PRESS

ATRIA

An Imprint of Simon & Schuster, LLC
1230 Avenue of the Americas
New York, NY 10020

First Primero Sueño Press/Atria Paperback edition July 2024

PRIMERO SUEÑO PRESS **/ ATRIA** PAPERBACK and colophon are trademarks of Simon & Schuster, LLC

Simon & Schuster: Celebrating 100 Years of Publishing in 2024

For information about special discounts for bulk purchases, please contact Simon & Schuster Special Sales at 1-866-506-1949 or business@simonandschuster.com.

The Simon & Schuster Speakers Bureau can bring authors to your live event. For more information or to book an event, contact the Simon & Schuster Speakers Bureau at 1-866-248-3049 or visit our website at www.simonspeakers.com.

Manufactured in the United States of America

3 5 7 9 10 8 6 4 2

Library of Congress Cataloging-in-Publication Data has been applied for.

ISBN 978-1-6680-7008-6
ISBN 978-1-6680-7072-7 (ebook)

The
LUCKY GIRL
JOURNAL

Belongs to _____

DOWNLOAD
the APP

WHERE TECHNOLOGY MEETS
INNER TRANSFORMATION

• Track Triggers

• Track Glimmers

• Check In with Feelings

• Journal Prompts

• Healing Exercises

• View Emotional Patterns over Time

DECLARATION
of INTENT

I,_____, pledge on this day to commit to
my journey of shaping my own luck and fostering personal growth.
I promise to fill this journal with bravery, positivity, and sincere
intentions. I acknowledge that I may face trials and challenges, but
these are the keystones of my resilience and strength. I embrace my
journey with an understanding that not every day will be a victory,
but every day is an opportunity. With this journal as my guide,
I am ready to tap into the well of luck within me and share this
abundance with the world.

_____

SIGNATURE

_____

START DATE

_____

COMPLETION DATE

Z

LUCK FINDS ITS WAY TO THOSE WHO DARE TO BELIEVE IN THE IMPOSSIBLE

PARTS

1. Introduction

2. Affirmations for Abundance

3. Exercises

4. Journal Prompts

5. Glimmer Tracking

Contents

1. INTRODUCTION

What Is the Lucky Girl Syndrome? 2

Self-Concept 3

The Lucky Girl Mindset 4

Ways to Cultivate Your Luck 5

Mind Reframing 7

2. AFFIRMATIONS FOR ABUNDANCE

Affirmations for Abundance Series 13

3. EXERCISES

Fill in the Blank 23

Long-Term Goals 41

Ideal Self 48

Replacing Limiting Beliefs 51

Lucky Moments 54

Wish Fulfilled 57

Gratitude Log 59

Strength Discovery 61

Overcoming Challenges 63

Daily Intentions & Reflections 66

4. JOURNAL PROMPTS

Journal Prompt Series 85

5. GLIMMER TRACKING

Glimmer Tracking Series 109

1
Introduction

What Is the Lucky Girl Syndrome?

Imagine waking up every day with an unfaltering belief that good things are coming your way. You walk through life with an air of confidence, knowing that you're destined for fortune, happiness, and success. This is what it means to be a "lucky girl." And before we go any further, I want to clarify what I mean when I refer to being a "lucky girl." I'm really speaking to everyone. This idea transcends gender; it's an energy, a mindset that anyone and everyone can embrace, regardless of who you are. And this belief, this mindset, is not something you're born with—it's something you can create for yourself. This journal will serve as a vessel for that creation. Through structured reflections, insights, affirmations, and exercises, if you allow it, it will guide you to discover, nurture, and cement this transformative belief in your daily life.

The journey ahead is not just about changing how you view the world; it's about changing how you view **yourself**. It's about the deep internal work that paves the way for external abundance. Each page will offer you the opportunity to delve deeper into your thoughts, desires, and beliefs, helping you gradually unlock your innate power to attract good fortune and luck. When we speak of abundance here, we're referring to creating an internal emotional temperament in which you have no sense of scarcity, alarm, or distrust. It's about experiencing richness and fulfillment in relationships, health, wealth, and every other aspect of your being. Even if the concept of abundance feels foreign or out of reach to you now, this journal will guide you on a trip of self-discovery and renewal, helping you realize that abundance is not just a possibility, but your birthright.

Self-Concept

Your self-concept is the mental image that you have of yourself. It encompasses your beliefs, thoughts, feelings, and experiences. It's how you perceive your capabilities, your identity, and your place in the world. This self-concept, when truly positive and nonjudgmental, has the power to transform your actions and reactions. It instills a sense of belief in yourself that invigorates your interactions with the world around you. Most importantly, it pushes you to build trust in the most important relationship you will ever have in life: the one with yourself. When you approach life with a potent sense of self, you radiate confidence that affects everyone and everything you encounter.

You already have a self-concept. But it may not be serving your fullest potential. Part of this journal will encourage you to reflect on your existing beliefs, thoughts, and values and determine areas where they can be recalibrated to elevate your self-concept. It extends to having a self-compassionate, realistic view of yourself—understanding what you are and aren't capable of in a sympathetic way. When you work on developing a fruitful self-concept, you start to see yourself as capable, worthy, and deserving of all the good things life has to offer. As a result, you begin to act in alignment with these beliefs. You make decisions and choices that reinforce this image of yourself. You hold your head high, make your voice heard, and live your life in a way that says, "I know who I am, I know what I want, and I deserve to achieve it." Your self-concept acts as the foundation of your worldview, affecting how you interpret events, make decisions, and interact with others. Cultivating an empowering self-concept involves practicing self-compassion and grace, which are essential components of finding yourself worthy. It's a practice of self-love that illuminates the road to success and contentment.

The Lucky Girl Mindset

The Lucky Girl Syndrome is about being in tune with yourself and the Divine. It's about recognizing that luck is not a random phenomenon but a force that you can attract by aligning your thoughts, feelings, and actions with positivity. When you see yourself as a magnet for good things, you naturally draw positive experiences toward yourself.

This syndrome is a shift in mindset, but more importantly, it's a shift in energy. It's a belief that you're constantly in sync with the attunement of your directed attentions and intentions, and that you're worthy of embodying your energy to its optimal potential. Each person has an energetic blueprint; like a fingerprint, but not visible to the eye. It's composed of patterns of your thought, life experiences, and intentions. It all radiates outward, communicating with your surroundings. By grounding your intentions in positivity and nurturing your inherent belief that good things are coming your way, you can attract positive outcomes. You understand that you are not at the mercy of chance or circumstances, but in fact, you have the power to create your own "luck."

This mindset transcends the surface of simple wishful thinking. It is a heartfelt declaration, a deeply rooted conviction, an unwavering belief in your inherent value and power to attract good luck and fortune into your life. You left for work but lost your car keys? Instead of going into panic mode, be lighthearted. Every glitch, like losing your keys, can open more than doors; it opens new paths. Every hiccup is a leap forward. A reminder that you're alive and things won't look or be the same every day. Embrace it, learn from it, grow from it. It requires an open mind, a receptive heart, and an unshakeable dedication to maintain this mindset despite external circumstances.

Ways to Cultivate Your Luck

❀ DREAM JOURNALING

❀ ABUNDANCE AFFIRMATIONS

❀ GLIMMER TRACKING

❀ MEDITATION AND VISUALIZATION

❀ BREATHWORK

❀ BEING OPEN-MINDED

❀ NOTICING THOUGHTS

❀ SAYING "THANK YOU"

❀ MOVING SOMATICALLY

❀ TAKING TIME FOR YOURSELF

The heart of a lucky person is an open door, welcoming change, embracing possibilities, and always daring to take the leap.

WHEN WE OPEN OURSELVES TO POSSIBILITY, WE BECOME MAGNETS FOR ABUNDANCE AND SERENDIPITY.

Mind Reframing

The process of mind reframing is an extremely powerful psychological tool. It involves shifting our perspectives and becoming aware of the growth opportunities in each experience. This reframing is integral to the Lucky Girl Syndrome, as it allows us to not just hope for the best, but to be a butterfly net for your thoughts, redirecting them so that they lead us into more beautiful experiences in life.

> *Remember, luck is simply abundance in disguise. It doesn't just fall from the sky, but comes to those who are willing to align their energy with the universe and keep their minds open to endless possibilities.*

When we reframe our minds, we let go of negative thought patterns that may have held us back. We replace fear and doubt with faith and optimism. We shift our perspective so we can see opportunities instead of obstacles. For example, seeing a breakup as an opportunity for growth instead of an obstacle of fear.

It's not just about thinking positively, but about believing positively. This mind reframing process changes our relationship with our desires and goals, allowing us to approach them with confidence. The beauty of mind reframing lies in its accessibility—it's a tool that anyone can use at any time, though it may require different approaches for different individuals. For some, simply thinking positively may not be enough; instead, reframing may involve acting positively or gradually shifting toward a positive outcome. This can look like exercising your body, getting a replenishing amount of sleep, setting and pursuing goals with determination, cultivating positive relationships, practicing gratitude, challenging negative thoughts, and acting mindfully and showing kindness to those around you. These actions not only demonstrate a positive belief in one's abilities but also contribute to a more optimistic outlook on life. This is particularly important for those who have experienced trauma, as their journey toward believing in positive changes may require grounding positivity in the familiar and witnessing the benefits of positive actions before their beliefs can begin to shift.

The Lucky Girl Syndrome does not encourage you to deny or avoid hardships altogether; rather, it encourages you to see them as stepping stones instead of stumbling blocks. Your response to life is the greatest power you hold, and this mindset moves you to harness the power of your response to life's inevitable challenges and changes. It's about consciously choosing an empowering narrative for your life—one where you are the fortunate protagonist navigating the world with confidence and optimism. A victim mindset sees challenges as obstacles that block progress, leaving you feeling powerless and stuck. In contrast, a warrior mindset views these same challenges as opportunities to demonstrate strength and resilience. Warriors take action, learn from their experiences, and emerge stronger, ready to face the next battle.

Mind reframing, or cognitive reframing as the scholars would have it, gifts us with this very power. It invites us to sit with our thoughts, to listen, to challenge, and finally, to change their tale. For example, you find yourself late for an important gathering. The insidious whisper of thoughts might chant, "You're late. They will judge you. It's a disaster." Anxiety flares, panic follows, and the tale spirals into chaos. Maybe you receive constructive criticism on a project you've poured your heart and soul into. Negative thoughts may swiftly invade your mind, whispering doubts about your abilities and the quality of your work. Your knee-jerk response might be to shut down and abandon the conversation altogether. These insidious thoughts can trigger feelings of inadequacy and self-doubt, making it challenging to process the feedback constructively and hindering your growth.

Negative interpretations quickly turn into self-destructive beliefs that permeate our thoughts, influence our emotions, and dictate our behaviors. They act as silent saboteurs, increasing our stress levels and diminishing our effectiveness in achieving our aspirations.

Now, consider the power of reframing. What if, instead, the internal monologue hums, "So you're late. It's not ideal, but it's hardly the end of the world. Apologize, catch up, and move forward." Suddenly, the tale shifts. The magnifying glass is lifted, and what seemed big and scary is just a minor setback. Panic gives way to acceptance, and chaos gracefully retreats.

> "The greatest discovery of all time is that a person can change his future by merely changing his attitude."
> —OPRAH WINFREY

In the theater of the mind, reframing empowers us to rewrite our internal scripts. It gives us the keys to the kingdom, allowing us to forge our own destinies rather than merely endure them. By doing so, it creates a ripple of change, beginning with our thoughts and eventually moving outward to our emotions, our actions, and our lives.

Consider receiving criticism at work. The initial thought may be, "I've failed." But a reframed thought might counter, "I have room to grow." The storm remains, but viewed through the lens of growth, it becomes less of a tempest and more of a nourishing rain.

Imagine you're at a social event, and you notice that someone you've been trying to get to know better hasn't engaged much with you. An automatic negative thought might be, "They must not like me or find me interesting." This thought could lead to feelings of rejection, sadness, or decreased self-esteem. However, by applying mind reframing, you might instead think, "They seem quiet tonight. Maybe they're tired, preoccupied, or dealing with some personal matters. Everyone has off days." This reframed thought helps you avoid personalizing the situation and reduces feelings of rejection. It encourages empathy and understanding. On the next page, you'll find more examples of mind reframing.

REFRAME THIS ⟶ TO THIS

WHY IS THIS HAPPENING TO ME? → WHAT IS THIS TEACHING ME?

IT'S TOO LATE. ⟶ IT'S NEVER TOO LATE TO START.

I AM DAMAGED. ⟶ I AM WHOLE AND COMPLETE.

I AM TIRED. ⟶ I AM FULL OF ENERGY.

I AM SICK. ⟶ HEALING ENERGY SURROUNDS MY BODY.

I AM A BURDEN. ⟶ I AM AN IMPORTANT PART OF MY COMMUNITY, FAMILY, AND SOCIETY.

I AM WORTHLESS. ⟶ I AM VALUABLE AND HAVE A PURPOSE.

I AM A DISAPPOINTMENT. ⟶ I CAN BE LOVED AND ACCEPTED.

I AM NOT CAPABLE. ⟶ I HAVE THE POWER TO SUCCEED.

I AM A MESS. ⟶ I AM HUMAN.

I AM SO ANGRY. ⟶ I HOLD SPACE FOR ANGER.

EVERYTHING IS MY FAULT. ⟶ I CAN LEARN FROM MY MISTAKES.

DESTRUCTIVE

JUMPING TO CONCLUSIONS

CATASTROPHIZING

OVERGENERALIZATION

LABELING

"SHOULD" STATEMENTS

PERSONALIZATION

BLAME

EMPOWERING

HAVING PRACTICAL GOALS

KEEPING AN OPEN MIND

PRACTICING MINDFULNESS

SEEKING OPPORTUNITY

SHOWING COMPASSION

CULTIVATING RESILIENCE

WARRIOR MINDSET

2
Affirmations
for Abundance

Affirmations

In this section, you will find a series of curated affirmations designed to enrich you with positivity and a profound sense of personal worth. With each affirmation spoken, you will step closer and closer to a more abundant and confident version of yourself.

As you explore these affirmations, allow yourself to embrace their meanings fully and let them resonate deeply within your spirit. You might find that they bring to light hidden strengths and inspire a renewed sense of purpose. Before beginning, take a moment to center yourself. Repeat any affirmations you feel hesitant to say or do not believe completely, and send love to each word you speak out loud. Visualize the words weaving through your daily actions and decisions, empowering you to manifest the reality you desire.

Affirmations for Abundance

My actions and thoughts are creating abundance in my life.

Every day, I am attracting more and more abundance.

My abundance is limitless.

I will always have enough.

The world is rigged in my favor.

I am the luckiest person I know.

Luck is my birthright.

Good things naturally gravitate toward me.

I give myself permission to receive new levels of love and abundance.

I appreciate the abundant opportunities that tomorrow brings.

Affirmations for
Attracting Wealth and Prosperity

I am open to prosperity in all its forms.

I am attracting wealth into my life now.

I am worthy of all the richness I desire.

Abundance flows easily when I relax and let it happen.

Prosperity is drawn to me, and I am open to receiving it.

I am thankful for the prosperity in my life.

I am aligned with the energy of wealth and prosperity.

*I now release all mental, emotional, and energetic blocks that are stopping me
from receiving and experiencing more prosperity in my life.*

Affirmations for Success and Career

I am surrounded by endless opportunities,
even if I don't see them immediately.

I am financially secure and free.

I am a magnet for success.

Every day, I invite opportunities into my life.

Everything I want always wants me more.

Everything always works in my favor.

My potential is limitless.

I am a thought leader in my industry.

I am in love with what I do.

Affirmations for Gratitude

I invite gratitude into my heart.

Every cell in my body vibrates with gratitude.

I am grateful for another chance to live my life.

I am able to see the good in each day.

Everything I did today is leading me to a better tomorrow.

My heart is open to receiving more than I could ever imagine.

I begin each day with an open heart.

I intentionally choose gratitude.

I am grateful for how far I have come.

Affirmations for Self-Belief

My potential is infinite.

I am deserving of all the good that comes my way.

Every day, my self-belief strengthens.

It is safe for me to be my authentic self.

I am powerful and in control of my reality.

I attract all that is good.

My life force energy is always full; I am never without it.

Everything I need is within me.

I am always guided toward my purpose.

I am the compass guiding all good things toward me.

I am energized and ready to tackle all challenges.

I am becoming the best version of myself.

Affirmations for Peace

Peace is my birthright, and I claim it now.

I appreciate the moments of connection and unity that bring people together in love and compassion.

I am grateful for each experience I witness.

Even if it doesn't always seem like it, everything is working out for me.

I have everything I need.

Things are getting better for me every day.

I embody pure love.

My inner peace attracts outer prosperity.

I am the epitome of calm in the face of life's storms.

I trust in the way my life is unfolding.

3

Exercises

Exercises

The process of priming your mind to recognize and create abundance all around you does not happen over a period of time and requires patience and practice. To help with this, it is recommended to set aside five to ten minutes each week to engage in a Lucky Girl Syndrome activity in this chapter. This will give you the opportunity to reflect on your self-concept intentionally and limiting beliefs and cultivate new, positive outlooks on yourself and life.

From fill-in-the-blank prompts that explore your deepest aspirations to visualization techniques that bring your goals to life in your mind's eye, each activity is designed to align your thoughts with the world's expansive generosity. Step by step, you'll find yourself not only hoping for but expecting and receiving more from the world around you.

Fill in the Blank

EXERCISE:

You'll see a series of sentences with certain words left out, indicated by a blank. Your mission is to fill in these blanks with words of your choice. These words could be nouns, verbs, adjectives, adverbs, or even names—it's totally up to you! The goal is to let your imagination run free and create unique sentences that reflect your personal experiences, ambitions, and positive thoughts.

WHY:

This exercise is based on the psychological principles of creativity and positive visualization. Creativity, being an inherent part of problem-solving, is key to overcoming obstacles and manifesting luck in our lives. By engaging your creativity in this way, you're training your brain to think outside of the box and see opportunities where others might only see challenges. The process of filling in the blanks encourages you to actively construct positive narratives about yourself and your life, a process known as positive visualization.

EXAMPLE:

When I woke up this morning, the first word that came to my mind was

_____ *newness* _____. One thing that makes me hopeful today

is ___ *the beautiful weather* ___. If I am faced with challenges, I will

___ *seek inner-resilience and strength* ___ to maintain my positive

mindset. Today, my top strength is _____ *unshakeable gratitude* _____.

In order to build my self-concept today, I want to

___ *affirm positive affirmations in the mirror* ___.

PART 1

My Lucky Day

One sunny morning, I woke up feeling incredibly

_____. I looked outside my window and saw

a(n) _____. I took it as a(n) _____ of the amazing

day ahead. I decided to go to my favorite place, _____.

There, I met a _____ who told me that I seemed like

a _____ person. They said, "You have an impressive

_____. Feeling _____,

I decided to try something new. I _____ for

the first time. It was a(n) _____ experience and

made me feel so _____. On my way home, I found

a(n) _____ on the ground. I picked it up, feeling

the _____ texture in my hand. This was the perfect

ending to my lucky day. That day, I learned that luck is

_____.

Reflection Questions

What emotions or experiences stood out most to you?

Trying something new can often lead to growth. What did you learn from this new experience?

PART 2

Cultivating Your Lucky Girl Mindset

When I woke up this morning, the first word that came to my mind was

_____. One thing that makes me

hopeful today is _____. If I am faced

with challenges, I will _____

to maintain my positive mindset. Today, my top strength is

_____. In order to build my self-concept

today, I want to _____

_____.

Reflection Questions

How does the first word that comes to your mind in the morning reflect your mindset and emotions?

How might you change or enhance this daily initial thought?

What personal attributes or achievements make you feel proud? Reflect on the areas of your life you're excited to improve.

PART 3

Cultivating Your Belief System

Something that doesn't serve me is _____, but

what truly uplifts me is _____. For some reason,

I always feel _____ when I

_____.

The greatest belief I have about myself is that I am

_____ and _____. In my

journey, I've learned that I am in control of my _____

_____ and capable of _____

_____. I am inviting _____ and _____

into my life.

Reflection Questions

In realizing that you are in control of certain aspects of your life, how does that knowledge contribute to your sense of self-efficacy and confidence?

How can you create more opportunities for experiences that uplift you?

PART 4

Growing Gratitude

Every day, I find reasons to be _____.

My heart fills with gratitude when I _____

_____. One unexpected thing I'm grateful for

is _____. Even when times are

tough, _____ reminds me to be grateful.

Cultivating a spirit of gratitude allows me to _____

_____.

Reflection Questions

In times of difficulty, what role does gratitude play for you?

How has cultivating a practice of gratitude influenced your interactions with others and your relationship with yourself?

PART 5

Confidence in Bloom

When I look in the mirror, I see a(n) _____

person. My inner _____ makes me

feel most confident. One thing I love about myself is my ability

to _____. I draw confidence from my

_____. By building confidence,

I am creating a(n) _____ future for myself.

Reflection Questions

Reflecting on your self-image, how has it evolved over time?

Think about the traits or abilities you love about yourself. How can you use these to further build your confidence and achieve your goals?

PART 6

The Power of Self-Belief

I feel most powerful when I _____. One thing

that reinforces my self-belief is _____.

A quote that strengthens my belief in myself is,

"_____

_____."

I have noticed that having a strong self-belief allows me to

_____. In the story of my life, I am

the _____.

Reflection Questions

Reflect on those moments when you feel most powerful. What common themes or elements can you identify in these moments?

How does that quote resonate with your personal experiences?

PART 7

The Well of Abundance

Abundance to me means _____

_____. I feel most

abundant when I _____. My life is rich

with _____ and _____.

I invite more abundance into my life by _____.

By acknowledging the abundance around me, I attract more

_____ into my life.

Reflection Questions

Expand on your personal definition of abundance. What does abundance mean to you?

What recurring factors contribute to when you feel the most abundance?

PART 8

The Lucky Charm

I consider my _____ to be my

lucky charm. A moment when I felt extremely lucky was when

_____.

I create my own luck by _____. One

habit that boosts my luck is _____. By

believing in my luck, I manifest _____

_____ in my life.

Reflection Questions

Expand on why you selected your personal lucky charm.

How have your actions contributed to your sense of fortune?

Long-Term Goals

EXERCISE:

Define your long-term goals clearly. This activity invites you to dive deep into your aspirations and outline your future in vivid detail. Now is your time to dream big and set your sights high. Start by brainstorming about the things you wish to bring into fruition in the next five years. What are your biggest dreams? What would you love to achieve? Don't hold back—no goal is too big or too small here. Think in terms of career, relationships, personal growth, health, and wealth.

WHY:

Setting clear, detailed goals is a critical first step toward achieving them. When you know exactly what you're working toward, you can better plan and direct your efforts. Plus, having a clear picture of your desired future can be incredibly motivating, helping you stay focused and persistent in the face of obstacles.

EXAMPLE:

GOAL:

Complete a 10k run within the next six months.

WHY? HOW WILL IT MAKE ME FEEL?

Running a 10k has been a dream of mine for years. It represents a significant milestone in my journey toward better health and fitness. Achieving this goal will make me feel accomplished, strong, and proud of myself. It will boost my confidence and reinforce my belief in my ability to set and achieve challenging physical goals.

STEPS TO TAKE:

Research training plans and join a local runner's group to stay accountable.

NOTES/IDEAS:

GOAL WORKSHEET

GOAL #1:

WHY? HOW WILL IT MAKE ME FEEL?

STEPS TO TAKE:

NOTES/IDEAS:

GOAL WORKSHEET

GOAL #2:

WHY? HOW WILL IT MAKE ME FEEL?

STEPS TO TAKE:

NOTES/IDEAS:

GOAL WORKSHEET

GOAL #3:

WHY? HOW WILL IT MAKE ME FEEL?

STEPS TO TAKE:

NOTES/IDEAS:

GOAL WORKSHEET

GOAL #4:

WHY? HOW WILL IT MAKE ME FEEL?

STEPS TO TAKE:

NOTES/IDEAS:

GOAL WORKSHEET

GOAL #5:

WHY? HOW WILL IT MAKE ME FEEL?

STEPS TO TAKE:

NOTES/IDEAS:

Ideal Self

EXERCISE:

Think of your future self, the person you aspire to become. This isn't about societal expectations or pressures, but rather your personal ideal future self. How do they behave? How do they think? What are their core beliefs and values? Jot down everything that comes to your mind. Consider different aspects of your ideal self, like emotional intelligence, communication style, personal strengths, habits, attitudes toward challenges, or any other facets that feel important to you.

Remember to approach this exercise with kindness and optimism. This is your ideal self, but it's important to appreciate the journey of becoming as much as the destination itself.

WHY:

This exercise is grounded in the concept of self-actualization, which is the innate need for personal growth and fulfillment. Imagining your ideal self can lead to a better alignment between your emotions and thoughts, helping you achieve a more integrated and coherent sense of identity. Visualization is a powerful tool for behavior change. When you regularly envision your ideal self, your subconscious will begin to align with this envisioned ideal, creating habits that support your desired personal growth and success.

EXAMPLE:

MY IDEAL SELF:

My ideal self is someone who embodies authenticity, kindness, and resilience. I am a confident individual who is unafraid to pursue my passions and dreams. In social interactions, I am calm, present, and fully aware of the other person's words and emotions. I always respond thoughtfully and ask questions. I am kind. I am confident in my responses and energized by bringing love to others through our interactions with each other. I handle stress and challenges gracefully and optimistically, and I don't take things too seriously. I always have my focus on doing the right thing.

ACTION STEPS:

Engage with my community through acts of selfless service. Look for opportunities that will challenge me to grow, like an ad hoc work project. Practice self-care daily by creating a ritual either in the morning or evening.

MY IDEAL SELF:

In order to envision your ideal self accordingly, describe the kind of person you want to embody. How do you dress? What do you like? What don't you like? What is your behavior like in different situations? What is your daily routine?

ACTION STEPS:

1.

2.

3.

4.

5.

Replacing Limiting Beliefs

EXERCISE:

This exercise invites you to examine the beliefs that may be holding you back, restricting your growth, or stifling your potential. Begin by identifying ten things that are holding you back or standing in the way of your goals. Analyze these self-limiting beliefs before consciously replacing them with positive and empowering ones.

WHY:

When you identify and modify self-limiting beliefs through this exercise, you can begin to change the way you interpret and respond to situations. This leads to improved emotional and behavioral outcomes in your life. Regularly catching these limiting beliefs and mindfully introducing better alternatives or a reframed version of this inner dialogue can help reinforce a sense of self-efficacy. It can modify the neural pathways in the brain that influence your positive thinking and resilience.

EXAMPLE:

Try to identify beliefs that are holding you back and reframe them into more empowering statements.

CURRENT BELIEF	REFRAMED BELIEF
My trust wound holds me back from building friendships.	The way I value trust helps me navigate positive and long-lasting friendships.

CURRENT BELIEF	REFRAMED BELIEF
I am so broke, I can't afford the life I want.	I am building a life of financial freedom so I can live the life I dream of.

CURRENT BELIEF	REFRAMED BELIEF
CURRENT BELIEF	REFRAMED BELIEF
CURRENT BELIEF	REFRAMED BELIEF

Lucky Moments

EXERCISE:

In this exercise, you will begin by taking a few moments to quiet your mind. Then, you will envision instances of luck and serendipity you want to happen in your life. These could be chance encounters that lead to amazing opportunities, unexpected successes, moments where everything just seems to fall into place, or any other scenarios that give you a sense of being favored and lucky. If you have trouble visualizing, scan the provided QR code below to access a guided meditation for imagining lucky moments.

WHY:

Visualizing your desired outcomes primes your brain to recognize and seize opportunities when they arise. It heightens your awareness, making you more likely to notice and capitalize on lucky moments when they happen. This exercise boosts your optimism and encourages you to adopt a perspective of abundance.

Visualization Meditation Example

EXPERIENCE 1

I'm sitting quietly in a peaceful garden, reflecting on the personal growth I've experienced over the past year. I visualize myself overcoming past fears and stepping out of my comfort zone. Each memory is vivid: speaking up in meetings, joining a dance class, and traveling alone for the first time. With each experience, I feel more confident and adventurous. I write about these milestones with a sense of gratitude and excitement for the future, recognizing that my transformation is ongoing and I am evolving for the better each day.

EXPERIENCE 2

I'm walking into a spacious, sunlit office, feeling a light breeze from the open windows. I'm greeted by warm smiles from my colleagues, who respect and value my contributions. As I sit down at my desk, I feel competent and excited about my projects. Throughout the day, I engage in meaningful work that aligns with my passions, including creative brainstorming sessions and impactful client meetings. I leave the office feeling fulfilled and appreciated, knowing that my work supports my growth and makes a positive difference.

EXPERIENCE 3

It's a lazy Sunday afternoon, and I'm in a cozy living room surrounded by my family. We're laughing over a board game, the room filled with light and warmth. I feel deeply connected to each person here, appreciating our differences and the love we share. I feel calm and grounded as we talk and play, assured by the strong bonds we've nurtured.

EXPERIENCE 4

I'm walking through a bustling street when I unexpectedly meet the person who would change my life forever. Our initial conversation flows effortlessly, filled with goofiness and shared interests. Over time, our connection deepens. Fast forward to our wedding day: it's a beautiful celebration, and we are surrounded by our closest family and friends. I feel grateful and excited for all our adventures, confident in our love and the life we will build together.

Visualization Meditation

EXPERIENCE 1

EXPERIENCE 2

EXPERIENCE 3

EXPERIENCE 4

Wish Fulfilled

EXERCISE:

Identify an expansive, all-encompassing wish that you have. This could be something that dramatically changes your life or brings you immense joy and satisfaction. Once you have that wish in mind, close your eyes and let your imagination flow.

Scan the QR code below to experience a visualization meditation to envision your ideal future self.

WHY:

By imagining your wish fulfilled, you are creating a detailed mental blueprint of what you want to achieve. This can clarify your desires, reinforce your commitment to them, and motivate you to take action toward achieving them.

IF MY WISH WAS FULFILLED RIGHT NOW, IT WOULD LOOK LIKE . . .

THE PERSON I AM WHEN MY WISH IS FULFILLED IS . . .

Gratitude Log

EXERCISE:

Set aside some quiet time for yourself to reflect on the things you're grateful for. These can be big or small, significant or trivial—the beauty lies in the appreciation of it all.

Write these moments of gratitude down in this dedicated space on the next page.

WHY:

Gratitude has been scientifically proven to boost happiness, reduce stress, and improve overall well-being. By focusing on what you're thankful for, you are consciously shifting your perspective from what's lacking in your life to what's abundant, thus cultivating an attitude of positivity and abundance. The act of writing enhances the gratitude experience, as it allows you to revisit and relive these moments of appreciation.

I AM SO GRATEFUL AND MY HEART FEELS SO FULL BECAUSE . . .

Strength Discovery

EXERCISE:

Take some quiet time to reflect upon your strengths—the unique traits and abilities that make you who you are. These strengths could be anything from kindness and empathy to resilience and creativity, or even specific skills like painting, public speaking, or problem-solving. Everyone has strengths, and they come in all forms. If you need additional help identifying your strengths, ask a friend or someone close to you for their feedback.

WHY:

By understanding your strengths, you can leverage them to overcome challenges, achieve your goals, and become the best version of yourself. This allows you to approach life's challenges with a strengths-based perspective, utilizing what you're good at to navigate difficulties. It encourages you to see yourself as capable and resourceful, thus enhancing your belief in your ability to make your own luck.

Try to identify your top strengths below. On the right, give evidence for these strengths.

STRENGTH ✊

EVIDENCE ♀

STRENGTH ✊

EVIDENCE ♀

STRENGTH ✊

EVIDENCE ♀

Overcoming Challenges

EXERCISE:

Write down the challenges you are currently facing. Be as detailed as you can. Don't dwell on the negatives, but allow yourself to acknowledge them. Remember, recognizing the challenge is the first step toward overcoming it.

WHY:

By writing down your challenges, you're taking the first step toward addressing them. This act alone can reduce feelings of overwhelm and help you see your situation more clearly. Articulating your challenges can provide insights into their root causes, which can be invaluable for resolving them. The brainstorming part of this exercise stimulates your creativity and critical thinking, key skills for problem-solving. It encourages you to see your challenges from different perspectives and come up with a wide range of potential solutions.

EXAMPLE:

CHALLENGE:	DISCOVERY:	SOLUTIONS:
I lost my mother.	I am not at peace with my grief.	I accept my grief and provide it with love and grace in order to move forward.

CHALLENGE #1:   DISCOVERY: SOLUTIONS:

CHALLENGE #2:   DISCOVERY: SOLUTIONS:

CHALLENGE #3:   DISCOVERY: SOLUTIONS:

CHALLENGE #4:   DISCOVERY: SOLUTIONS:

Daily Intentions & Reflections

EXERCISE:

Take a few moments to build gratitude and set your intentions for your life. These intentions should be guiding principles that you want to live by, actions you want to take, or feelings you want to cultivate.

At the end of the day, spend a few moments reflecting on your day. How did your intentions guide your actions? Did you notice any change in your energy, mindset, or behavior? Write down these reflections.

WHY:

This exercise encourages a proactive, intentional, and reflective approach to life, all essential elements of the Lucky Girl Mindset. It helps you see that you are not just a passive recipient of luck, but an active creator of it through your intentions and actions.

Morning EXAMPLE

DATE: _____

LOOK UP AND GIVE GRATITUDE FOR THE SMALL THINGS IN LIFE.
WRITE DOWN THREE THINGS YOU ARE GRATEFUL FOR.

I am grateful for my home.
I am grateful for the sun.
I am grateful for this journal.

VISUALIZE YOUR DREAM LIFE AND MAKE THE INTENTION TO CREATE A
GREAT DAY. WRITE THREE THINGS YOU WISH TO ACCOMPLISH TODAY.

I will have a productive work session.
I will work out hard and eat a nutritious dinner.
I will text a friend to see how they are doing.

HOW WILL YOU SHOW YOURSELF LOVE TODAY?

By drinking lots of water and thinking kind thoughts.

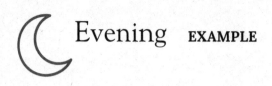 Evening **EXAMPLE**

TODAY MADE ME FEEL

BECAUSE . . .

I woke up with energy and made myself a smoothie.
I got lots of work done but started feeling sluggish
at 2:00 p.m., so I drank a glass of water and sat
outside in the sun.

HOW WAS MY ENERGY TODAY? WHAT DID I LEARN?

I learned to pay attention to my body and rest for a
moment. This brought my energy back up later in
the day and I did not feel burnt out. My energy was
positive.

FEELINGS, REFLECTIONS, OR NOTES . . .

It felt amazing to be outside and breathe fresh
air. I've been so cooped up indoors, and I realize it's
important to walk or sit outside—it almost feels
like I'm stepping out of my head and entering the
present world.

Morning

DATE: _____

LOOK UP AND GIVE GRATITUDE FOR THE SMALL THINGS IN LIFE.
WRITE DOWN THREE THINGS YOU ARE GRATEFUL FOR.

VISUALIZE YOUR DREAM LIFE AND MAKE THE INTENTION TO CREATE A
GREAT DAY. WRITE THREE THINGS YOU WISH TO ACCOMPLISH TODAY.

HOW WILL YOU SHOW YOURSELF LOVE TODAY?

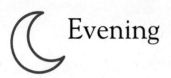 Evening

TODAY MADE ME FEEL

BECAUSE . . .

HOW WAS MY ENERGY TODAY? WHAT DID I LEARN?

FEELINGS, REFLECTIONS, OR NOTES . . .

Morning

DATE: _____

LOOK UP AND GIVE GRATITUDE FOR THE SMALL THINGS IN LIFE.
WRITE DOWN THREE THINGS YOU ARE GRATEFUL FOR.

VISUALIZE YOUR DREAM LIFE AND MAKE THE INTENTION TO CREATE A
GREAT DAY. WRITE THREE THINGS YOU WISH TO ACCOMPLISH TODAY.

HOW WILL YOU SHOW YOURSELF LOVE TODAY?

 Evening

TODAY MADE ME FEEL

BECAUSE . . .

HOW WAS MY ENERGY TODAY? WHAT DID I LEARN?

FEELINGS, REFLECTIONS, OR NOTES . . .

Morning

DATE: _____

LOOK UP AND GIVE GRATITUDE FOR THE SMALL THINGS IN LIFE.
WRITE DOWN THREE THINGS YOU ARE GRATEFUL FOR.

VISUALIZE YOUR DREAM LIFE AND MAKE THE INTENTION TO CREATE A
GREAT DAY. WRITE THREE THINGS YOU WISH TO ACCOMPLISH TODAY.

HOW WILL YOU SHOW YOURSELF LOVE TODAY?

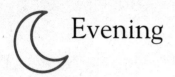 Evening

TODAY MADE ME FEEL

BECAUSE . . .

HOW WAS MY ENERGY TODAY? WHAT DID I LEARN?

FEELINGS, REFLECTIONS, OR NOTES . . .

Morning

DATE: _____

LOOK UP AND GIVE GRATITUDE FOR THE SMALL THINGS IN LIFE.
WRITE DOWN THREE THINGS YOU ARE GRATEFUL FOR.

VISUALIZE YOUR DREAM LIFE AND MAKE THE INTENTION TO CREATE A
GREAT DAY. WRITE THREE THINGS YOU WISH TO ACCOMPLISH TODAY.

HOW WILL YOU SHOW YOURSELF LOVE TODAY?

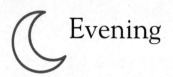 Evening

TODAY MADE ME FEEL

BECAUSE . . .

HOW WAS MY ENERGY TODAY? WHAT DID I LEARN?

FEELINGS, REFLECTIONS, OR NOTES . . .

Morning

DATE: _____

LOOK UP AND GIVE GRATITUDE FOR THE SMALL THINGS IN LIFE.
WRITE DOWN THREE THINGS YOU ARE GRATEFUL FOR.

VISUALIZE YOUR DREAM LIFE AND MAKE THE INTENTION TO CREATE A
GREAT DAY. WRITE THREE THINGS YOU WISH TO ACCOMPLISH TODAY.

HOW WILL YOU SHOW YOURSELF LOVE TODAY?

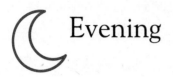 Evening

TODAY MADE ME FEEL

BECAUSE . . .

HOW WAS MY ENERGY TODAY? WHAT DID I LEARN?

FEELINGS, REFLECTIONS, OR NOTES . . .

Morning

DATE: _____

LOOK UP AND GIVE GRATITUDE FOR THE SMALL THINGS IN LIFE.
WRITE DOWN THREE THINGS YOU ARE GRATEFUL FOR.

VISUALIZE YOUR DREAM LIFE AND MAKE THE INTENTION TO CREATE A
GREAT DAY. WRITE THREE THINGS YOU WISH TO ACCOMPLISH TODAY.

HOW WILL YOU SHOW YOURSELF LOVE TODAY?

 Evening

TODAY MADE ME FEEL

BECAUSE . . .

HOW WAS MY ENERGY TODAY? WHAT DID I LEARN?

FEELINGS, REFLECTIONS, OR NOTES . . .

Morning

DATE: _____

LOOK UP AND GIVE GRATITUDE FOR THE SMALL THINGS IN LIFE.
WRITE DOWN THREE THINGS YOU ARE GRATEFUL FOR.

VISUALIZE YOUR DREAM LIFE AND MAKE THE INTENTION TO CREATE A
GREAT DAY. WRITE THREE THINGS YOU WISH TO ACCOMPLISH TODAY.

HOW WILL YOU SHOW YOURSELF LOVE TODAY?

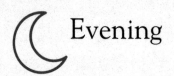 Evening

TODAY MADE ME FEEL

BECAUSE . . .

HOW WAS MY ENERGY TODAY? WHAT DID I LEARN?

FEELINGS, REFLECTIONS, OR NOTES . . .

Morning

DATE: _____

LOOK UP AND GIVE GRATITUDE FOR THE SMALL THINGS IN LIFE.
WRITE DOWN THREE THINGS YOU ARE GRATEFUL FOR.

VISUALIZE YOUR DREAM LIFE AND MAKE THE INTENTION TO CREATE A
GREAT DAY. WRITE THREE THINGS YOU WISH TO ACCOMPLISH TODAY.

HOW WILL YOU SHOW YOURSELF LOVE TODAY?

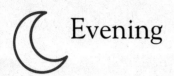 Evening

TODAY MADE ME FEEL

BECAUSE . . .

HOW WAS MY ENERGY TODAY? WHAT DID I LEARN?

FEELINGS, REFLECTIONS, OR NOTES . . .

4

Journal Prompts

Journal Prompts

In this chapter, you'll find a series of journal prompts designed to help you explore your thoughts, feelings, and beliefs. Each prompt is aimed to push you a little bit outside of your comfort zone and inspire you to reflect deeply. Journaling is more than just recording events; it's an intimate dialogue with your inner self. You might be surprised by the profound insights that emerge when you give your inner voice a place to speak.

For each prompt, take some time to really think about your answer before you begin writing. Don't rush. Let your thoughts flow freely onto the page, and remember, there are no wrong answers. These are your thoughts, your feelings, your beliefs.

By engaging with these prompts, you're exploring different aspects of your personality, experiences, and aspirations. This can help you gain insights about yourself that you may not have been aware of and allows you to track your personal growth over time.

A Sense of Gratitude

DESCRIBE A MOMENT WHEN YOU EXPERIENCED A SENSE
OF GRATITUDE OR APPRECIATION FOR SOMETHING SMALL OR
SEEMINGLY INSIGNIFICANT.

@zenfulnote DATE: / / /

A Belief That Has Evolved

WHAT IS A BELIEF OR PERSPECTIVE OF YOURS THAT HAS CHANGED
OVER TIME? WHAT SPARKED THAT CHANGE?

@zenfulnote   Zenfulnote   DATE: /   /   /

The Color of Your Joy

WHAT COLOR IS YOUR JOY? WHY?

Feeling Alive

DESCRIBE A MOMENT WHEN YOU FELT TRULY ALIVE AND PRESENT IN THE MOMENT.

A Personal Goal

WHAT IS SOMETHING THAT YOU HAVE ALWAYS WANTED TO DO
BUT HAVEN'T HAD THE OPPORTUNITY TO DO YET? WHY IS IT
IMPORTANT TO YOU?

@zenfulnote   Zenfulnote   DATE: /   /   /

Clarity

WRITE ABOUT A MOMENT WHEN YOU EXPERIENCED
A SENSE OF CLARITY.

A Positive Influence

DESCRIBE A PERSON WHO HAS BEEN A POSITIVE INFLUENCE IN YOUR LIFE. HOW HAVE THEY IMPACTED YOU, AND WHAT HAVE YOU LEARNED FROM THEM?

The Color of Your Love

WHAT COLOR IS YOUR LOVE? WHY?

Your Success

REFLECT ON AND EXPRESS GRATITUDE FOR YOUR
ACCOMPLISHMENTS AND SUCCESSES.

Your Biggest Dream

WHAT IS A GOAL OR DREAM THAT YOU'VE HAD FOR A LONG TIME?
WHAT STEPS CAN YOU TAKE TO MAKE THAT GOAL A REALITY?

A Recent Challenge

WHAT IS SOMETHING THAT HAS CHALLENGED YOU RECENTLY, AND HOW HAVE YOU GROWN FROM IT?

@zenfulnote   Zenfulnote   DATE: /   /   /

Your Lucky Self

WHAT DOES YOUR LUCKY SELF LOOK LIKE, AND HOW CAN YOU
EMBODY THAT VERSION OF YOU DAILY?

@zenfulnote   Zenfulnote   DATE: /   /   /

Self-Love

WHAT ARE THREE THINGS THAT YOU LOVE ABOUT YOURSELF
AND WHY?

Living Lucky

IN WHAT WAYS ARE YOU ALREADY LIVING AS YOUR LUCKY SELF?

Gratitude

HOW CAN YOU BETTER EXPRESS GRATITUDE IN YOUR DAILY LIFE?

@zenfulnote Zenfulnote DATE: / / /

Values

WHAT ARE THE PERSONAL VALUES THAT GUIDE YOUR DECISIONS AND ACTIONS?

Positive Habits

WHAT ARE THE POSITIVE HABITS YOU WANT TO CULTIVATE IN THE
UPCOMING MONTHS?

Positive Changes

WHAT ARE SOME POSITIVE CHANGES YOU'VE NOTICED IN
YOURSELF RECENTLY?

Define Success

WHAT IS YOUR PERSONAL DEFINITION OF SUCCESS?

Regulating Stress

HOW CAN YOU BETTER MANAGE STRESS IN YOUR LIFE?

Reacting to Setbacks

HOW DOES YOUR LUCKY SELF REACT TO FAILURE OR SETBACKS?

Living Authentically

WHAT DOES LIVING AUTHENTICALLY MEAN TO YOU, AND HOW
ARE YOU PURSUING IT?

@zenfulnote Zenfulnote   DATE: /   /   /

5
Glimmer Tracking

Glimmer Tracking

As you journey through life, it's easy to overlook the small, fleeting moments of joy and wonder—those little glimmers that shine brightly against the backdrop of daily routines. This chapter introduces you to the art of Glimmer Tracking, a practice designed to help you capture and cherish these brief instances of happiness and insight. By keeping a record of these moments, you create a treasure trove of positivity that can uplift and inspire you, especially during challenging times.

Glimmer Tracking is a reflective process that teaches you to be present and attentive to the nuances of your daily life. As you begin to observe and document these glimmers, you'll notice patterns and themes that may have previously eluded you. This awareness brings a deeper understanding of what truly nourishes your spirit and fuels your joy.

When we track glimmers, we are essentially savoring positive experiences.

Want to track your glimmers on the go? Download the Zenfulnote app.

TRACK YOUR GLIMMERS

EVENT
In detail, describe what happened.

FEELINGS
How did it make you feel?

GLIMMER ECHO
How did this glimmer spark a chain of positivity?

GLIMMER ESSENCE
What is the core reason this felt like a glimmer to you?

TRACK YOUR GLIMMERS

EVENT
In detail, describe what happened.

FEELINGS
How did it make you feel?

GLIMMER ECHO
How did this glimmer spark a chain of positivity?

GLIMMER ESSENCE
What is the core reason this felt like a glimmer to you?

TRACK YOUR GLIMMERS

EVENT
In detail, describe what happened.

FEELINGS
How did it make you feel?

GLIMMER ECHO
How did this glimmer spark a chain of positivity?

GLIMMER ESSENCE
What is the core reason this felt like a glimmer to you?

TRACK YOUR GLIMMERS

EVENT
In detail, describe what happened.

FEELINGS
How did it make you feel?

GLIMMER ECHO
How did this glimmer spark a chain of positivity?

GLIMMER ESSENCE
What is the core reason this felt like a glimmer to you?

TRACK YOUR GLIMMERS

EVENT
In detail, describe what happened.

FEELINGS
How did it make you feel?

GLIMMER ECHO
How did this glimmer spark a chain of positivity?

GLIMMER ESSENCE
What is the core reason this felt like a glimmer to you?

TRACK YOUR GLIMMERS

EVENT
In detail, describe what happened.

FEELINGS
How did it make you feel?

GLIMMER ECHO
How did this glimmer spark a chain of positivity?

GLIMMER ESSENCE
What is the core reason this felt like a glimmer to you?

TRACK YOUR GLIMMERS

EVENT
In detail, describe what happened.

FEELINGS
How did it make you feel?

GLIMMER ECHO
How did this glimmer spark a chain of positivity?

GLIMMER ESSENCE
What is the core reason this felt like a glimmer to you?

TRACK YOUR GLIMMERS

EVENT
In detail, describe what happened.

FEELINGS
How did it make you feel?

GLIMMER ECHO
How did this glimmer spark a chain of positivity?

GLIMMER ESSENCE
What is the core reason this felt like a glimmer to you?

TRACK YOUR GLIMMERS

EVENT
In detail, describe what happened.

FEELINGS
How did it make you feel?

GLIMMER ECHO
How did this glimmer spark a chain of positivity?

GLIMMER ESSENCE
What is the core reason this felt like a glimmer to you?

TRACK YOUR GLIMMERS

EVENT
In detail, describe what happened.

FEELINGS
How did it make you feel?

GLIMMER ECHO
How did this glimmer spark a chain of positivity?

GLIMMER ESSENCE
What is the core reason this felt like a glimmer to you?

TRACK YOUR GLIMMERS

EVENT
In detail, describe what happened.

FEELINGS
How did it make you feel?

GLIMMER ECHO
How did this glimmer spark a chain of positivity?

GLIMMER ESSENCE
What is the core reason this felt like a glimmer to you?

TRACK YOUR GLIMMERS

EVENT
In detail, describe what happened.

FEELINGS
How did it make you feel?

GLIMMER ECHO
How did this glimmer spark a chain of positivity?

GLIMMER ESSENCE
What is the core reason this felt like a glimmer to you?

TRACK YOUR GLIMMERS

EVENT
In detail, describe what happened.

FEELINGS
How did it make you feel?

GLIMMER ECHO
How did this glimmer spark a chain of positivity?

GLIMMER ESSENCE
What is the core reason this felt like a glimmer to you?

TRACK YOUR GLIMMERS

EVENT
In detail, describe what happened.

FEELINGS
How did it make you feel?

GLIMMER ECHO
How did this glimmer spark a chain of positivity?

GLIMMER ESSENCE
What is the core reason this felt like a glimmer to you?

TRACK YOUR GLIMMERS

EVENT
In detail, describe what happened.

FEELINGS
How did it make you feel?

GLIMMER ECHO
How did this glimmer spark a chain of positivity?

GLIMMER ESSENCE
What is the core reason this felt like a glimmer to you?

TRACK YOUR GLIMMERS

EVENT
In detail, describe what happened.

FEELINGS
How did it make you feel?

GLIMMER ECHO
How did this glimmer spark a chain of positivity?

GLIMMER ESSENCE
What is the core reason this felt like a glimmer to you?

TRACK YOUR GLIMMERS

EVENT
In detail, describe what happened.

FEELINGS
How did it make you feel?

GLIMMER ECHO
How did this glimmer spark a chain of positivity?

GLIMMER ESSENCE
What is the core reason this felt like a glimmer to you?

TRACK YOUR GLIMMERS

EVENT
In detail, describe what happened.

FEELINGS
How did it make you feel?

GLIMMER ECHO
How did this glimmer spark a chain of positivity?

GLIMMER ESSENCE
What is the core reason this felt like a glimmer to you?

TRACK YOUR GLIMMERS

EVENT
In detail, describe what happened.

FEELINGS
How did it make you feel?

GLIMMER ECHO
How did this glimmer spark a chain of positivity?

GLIMMER ESSENCE
What is the core reason this felt like a glimmer to you?

TRACK YOUR GLIMMERS

EVENT
In detail, describe what happened.

FEELINGS
How did it make you feel?

GLIMMER ECHO
How did this glimmer spark a chain of positivity?

GLIMMER ESSENCE
What is the core reason this felt like a glimmer to you?

TRACK YOUR GLIMMERS

EVENT
In detail, describe what happened.

FEELINGS
How did it make you feel?

GLIMMER ECHO
How did this glimmer spark a chain of positivity?

GLIMMER ESSENCE
What is the core reason this felt like a glimmer to you?

TRACK YOUR GLIMMERS

EVENT
In detail, describe what happened.

FEELINGS
How did it make you feel?

GLIMMER ECHO
How did this glimmer spark a chain of positivity?

GLIMMER ESSENCE
What is the core reason this felt like a glimmer to you?

TRACK YOUR GLIMMERS

EVENT
In detail, describe what happened.

FEELINGS
How did it make you feel?

GLIMMER ECHO
How did this glimmer spark a chain of positivity?

GLIMMER ESSENCE
What is the core reason this felt like a glimmer to you?

TRACK YOUR GLIMMERS

EVENT
In detail, describe what happened.

FEELINGS
How did it make you feel?

GLIMMER ECHO
How did this glimmer spark a chain of positivity?

GLIMMER ESSENCE
What is the core reason this felt like a glimmer to you?

TRACK YOUR GLIMMERS

EVENT
In detail, describe what happened.

FEELINGS
How did it make you feel?

GLIMMER ECHO
How did this glimmer spark a chain of positivity?

GLIMMER ESSENCE
What is the core reason this felt like a glimmer to you?

TRACK YOUR GLIMMERS

EVENT
In detail, describe what happened.

FEELINGS
How did it make you feel?

GLIMMER ECHO
How did this glimmer spark a chain of positivity?

GLIMMER ESSENCE
What is the core reason this felt like a glimmer to you?

TRACK YOUR GLIMMERS

EVENT
In detail, describe what happened.

FEELINGS
How did it make you feel?

GLIMMER ECHO
How did this glimmer spark a chain of positivity?

GLIMMER ESSENCE
What is the core reason this felt like a glimmer to you?

TRACK YOUR GLIMMERS

EVENT
In detail, describe what happened.

FEELINGS
How did it make you feel?

GLIMMER ECHO
How did this glimmer spark a chain of positivity?

GLIMMER ESSENCE
What is the core reason this felt like a glimmer to you?

TRACK YOUR GLIMMERS

EVENT
In detail, describe what happened.

FEELINGS
How did it make you feel?

GLIMMER ECHO
How did this glimmer spark a chain of positivity?

GLIMMER ESSENCE
What is the core reason this felt like a glimmer to you?

TRACK YOUR GLIMMERS

EVENT
In detail, describe what happened.

FEELINGS
How did it make you feel?

GLIMMER ECHO
How did this glimmer spark a chain of positivity?

GLIMMER ESSENCE
What is the core reason this felt like a glimmer to you?

TRACK YOUR GLIMMERS

EVENT
In detail, describe what happened.

FEELINGS
How did it make you feel?

GLIMMER ECHO
How did this glimmer spark a chain of positivity?

GLIMMER ESSENCE
What is the core reason this felt like a glimmer to you?

TRACK YOUR GLIMMERS

EVENT
In detail, describe what happened.

FEELINGS
How did it make you feel?

GLIMMER ECHO
How did this glimmer spark a chain of positivity?

GLIMMER ESSENCE
What is the core reason this felt like a glimmer to you?

TRACK YOUR GLIMMERS

EVENT
In detail, describe what happened.

FEELINGS
How did it make you feel?

GLIMMER ECHO
How did this glimmer spark a chain of positivity?

GLIMMER ESSENCE
What is the core reason this felt like a glimmer to you?

DOWNLOAD
the APP

WHERE TECHNOLOGY MEETS
INNER TRANSFORMATION

• Track Triggers

• Track Glimmers

• Check In with Feelings

• Journal Prompts

• Healing Exercises

• View Emotional Patterns over Time